W9-BIU-815

SNOWBOARDING

BY JOHN HAMILTON

A&D Xtreme
An imprint of Abdo Publishing | www.abdopublishing.com

Visit us at
www.abdopublishing.com

Published by Abdo Publishing Company, a division of ABDO, PO Box 398166, Minneapolis, Minnesota 55439. Copyright ©2015 by Abdo Consulting Group, Inc. International copyrights reserved in all countries. No part of this book may be reproduced in any form without written permission from the publisher. A&D Xtreme™ is a trademark and logo of Abdo Publishing Company.

Printed in the United States of America, North Mankato, Minnesota.
042014
092014

 PRINTED ON RECYCLED PAPER

Editor: Sue Hamilton
Graphic Design: Sue Hamilton
Cover Design: John Hamilton
Cover Photo: Thinkstock
Interior Photos: AP-pgs 7, 8 (right), 9, 12, 14, 15, 16-17, 23 (top right), 24-25 & 27 (bottom left & right); Blair Snow-pg 24 (halfpipe diagram); Brunswick Corp-pg 6; Corbis-pgs 4-5 & 28-29; Getty Images-pgs 8, 13, 26, 27 (top); Hans Henning Wenk-pgs 18-19; K2 Sports USA-pgs 21, 22 & 30-31; Thinkstock-pgs 1, 2-3, 10-11, 20, 23 (top left and bottom) & 32; Vailads-pg 8 (snowboard diagram).

Websites
To learn more about Action Sports, visit booklinks.abdopublishing.com. These links are routinely monitored and updated to provide the most current information available.

Library of Congress Control Number: 2014932226

Cataloging-in-Publication Data

Hamilton, John.
 Snowboarding / John Hamilton.
   p. cm. -- (Action sports)
Includes index.
ISBN 978-1-62403-444-2
1. Snowboarding--Juvenile literature.   I. Title.
796.93--dc23

2014932226

CONTENTS

SNOWBOARDING

Take an epic snow run and mix in the dangers of surfing and the craziest tricks of skateboarding and you've got the sport of snowboarding. It started as an annoying little brother on the ski slopes, but it never left. Before long, the airdogs, hotdogs, shredders, and boarders made it one of the wildest sports on snow.

Xtreme Quote: "Snowboarding is falling. Just a matter of whether you are controlling the fall, or the fall is controlling you." –Anonymous

HISTORY

In the early 1960s, Sherman Poppen tied two skis together for his kids to glide down snow-covered hills. He went on to create the "Snurfer" (snow and surfer). He sold the board's design to Brunswick Corporation in 1965. Millions of Snurfers were sold over the next two decades. The first national Snurfing competition took place in 1978 in Muskegon, Michigan.

A 1960s ad for the Snurfer.

Over the years, enthusiasts in Snurfing, skiing, skateboarding, and surfing worked on new board designs. By the late 1970s, the snowboard was born. The first World Championships were held in 1983. The International Snowboard Federation was formed in 1989. The ISF gave way to the World Snowboard Federation in 2002. The sport entered the Winter Olympic Games in 1998.

In 1998, Ross Rebagliati of Canada won the men's giant slalom snowboarding event at the Winter Olympic Games in Nagano, Japan. He was the first athlete to win a gold medal in snowboarding.

BOARDS

Snowboards are designed according to riding style. There are several different types.

Freeride or all-mountain boards are the most popular. These are used for general riding. The tail is narrow, shorter, and flatter than the nose of the board.

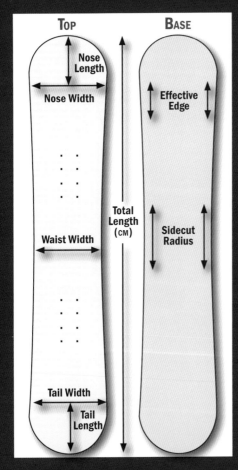

TOP

BASE

Nose Length

Nose Width

Effective Edge

Total Length (CM)

Waist Width

Sidecut Radius

Tail Width

Tail Length

Freestyle snowboards are shorter, wider, and more stable. Many beginners use freestyle snowboards. They are also used when performing tricks.

Carving snowboards, also known as alpine and race boards, are narrower and longer. These allow riders to get faster speeds and cleaner curves.

CLOTHING & GEAR

Snowboarders dress for warmth, but if they get overheated, sweat can freeze on their skin. They must also be able to move. Most people dress in layers.

A snowboarder starts with thermal underwear and padded snowboarding socks. A second layer consists of a sweater or fleece jacket, snowboarding pants, and snowboarding boots with bindings that connect to the board. The outside layer includes a hat and helmet, goggles, a snowboarding jacket, and gloves. By layering, snowboarders can remove top layers if they get too hot.

FREERIDE & FREECARVE

There are several styles of snowboarding. Freeride snowboarding is simply riding down a mountain. Beginners start with this style. Sounds easy? Be prepared to fall a lot! Advanced snowboarders take it to the extreme, going down vertical drops and traveling wherever they want to go.

Freecarve is for riders with a need for speed. Freecarvers move down the mountain at full throttle, carving or sliding in an arc. It takes focus to stay in control and safe when moving so fast.

FREESTYLE

Flip

Tricks are performed in freestyle snowboarding. Riders perform at parks, mountains, and towns. Jumps, spins, flips, grabs, halfpipes, and rails are all part of the sport. Freestyle snowboards are shorter, lighter, and easier to maneuver over the snow. The tail and tip are identical in shape.

Grab

Halfpipe

Riding a Rail

Spin

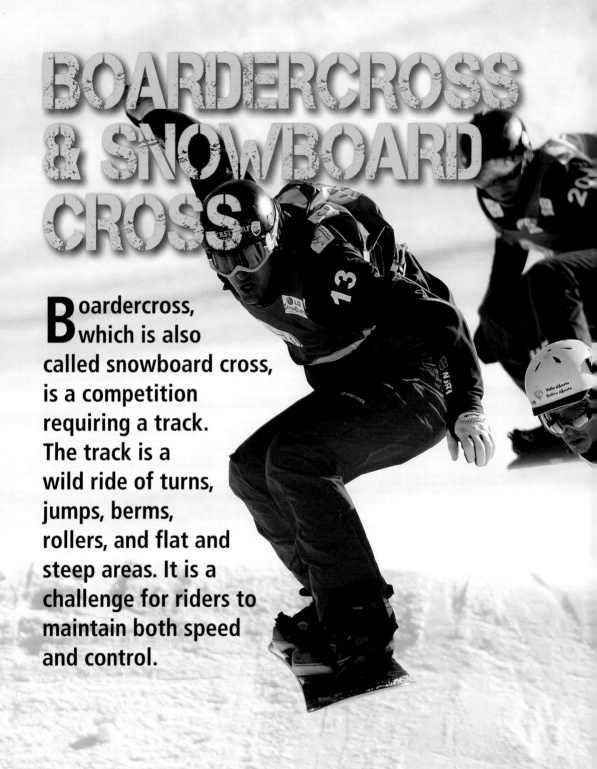

BOARDERCROSS & SNOWBOARD CROSS

Boardercross, which is also called snowboard cross, is a competition requiring a track. The track is a wild ride of turns, jumps, berms, rollers, and flat and steep areas. It is a challenge for riders to maintain both speed and control.

Four to six riders start at one time, each racing to be the fastest to cross the finish line. The fastest boarders go on to race again, until the final round determines the ultimate winner.

Xtreme Fact: Boardercross is the snowy equivalent of motorcycle racing's motocross.

ALPINE SNOWBOARDING

Alpine snowboarding is a race down the hill using clean, controlled turns on smooth terrain.

Snowboarders use stiff boards and rigid boots for precision carving. The sport is also known as hardbooting.

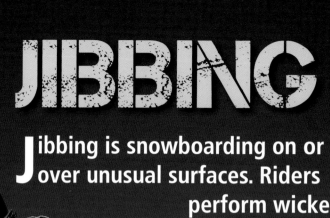

JIBBING

Jibbing is snowboarding on or over unusual surfaces. Riders perform wicked tricks on metal rails, tables, trees, rocks, benches, ledges, walls, even vehicles and people.

Xtreme Fact: A snowboard used for jibbing is sometimes called a jibstick.

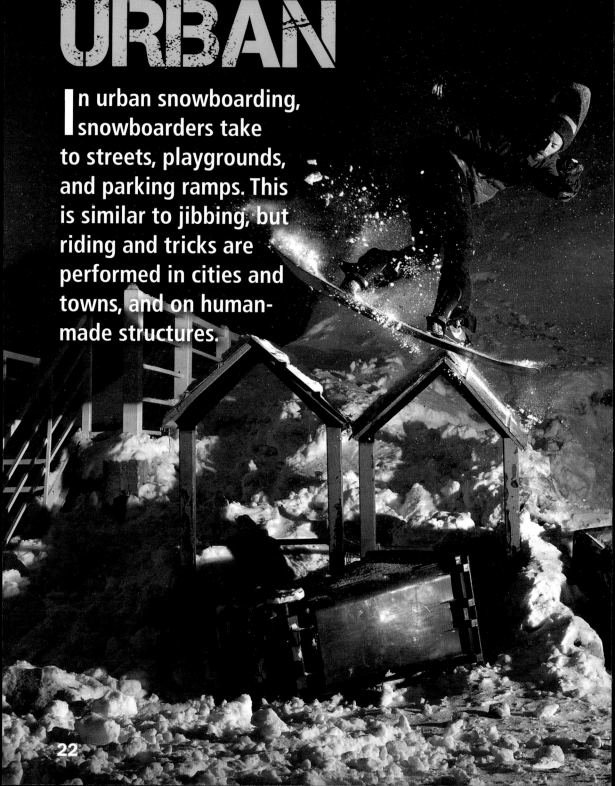

URBAN

In urban snowboarding, snowboarders take to streets, playgrounds, and parking ramps. This is similar to jibbing, but riding and tricks are performed in cities and towns, and on human-made structures.

HALFPIPE

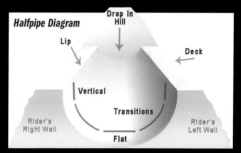

A halfpipe is a huge, U-shaped, snow-covered surface for going airborne and achieving gravity-defying tricks. Early halfpipes were simply earth-lined gullies covered in snow. Today's pipes are carefully built, groomed, and maintained. Halfpipe competition made it into the Winter Olympic Games in 1998.

Benjamin Farrow performs a trick during the 2013 World Cup U.S. Grand Prix halfpipe snowboarding finals in Frisco, Colorado.

X GAMES

The exciting Winter X Games feature the action sports of skiing, snowmobiling, and snowboarding. Both men and women compete. Snowboarders compete in slopestyle, superpipe, big air, and snowboard street.

Ståle Sandbech of Norway competes in the men's snowboard slopestyle at the 2014 Winter X Games in Aspen, Colorado.

Kelly Clark competes in the X Games women's superpipe in 2014.

The X Games are broadcast each year by ESPN and feature some of the best snowboarders in the world.

Kevin Pearce launches into a practice run for the big air competition at the 2009 Winter X Games.

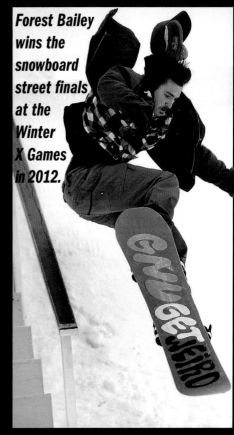

Forest Bailey wins the snowboard street finals at the Winter X Games in 2012.

WINTER OLYMPICS

The sport of snowboarding first appeared in the Winter Olympic Games in 1998 in Japan. Snowboarders competed in the giant slalom and halfpipe. In the 2014 Winter Olympic Games in Sochi, Russia, men and women snowboarders competed in the giant slalom, halfpipe, snowboard cross, snowboard slopestyle, and parallel slalom.

USA's Sage Kotsenburg won the first Olympic gold medal in men's snowboard slopestyle in 2014. The United States has won more gold medals in snowboarding than any other country.

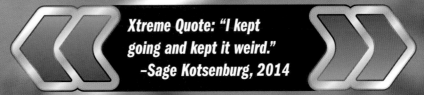

Xtreme Quote: "I kept going and kept it weird." –Sage Kotsenburg, 2014

GLOSSARY

Airdogs
A snowboarder who does jumps and aerial tricks.

Berm
A wall of snow built up in a corner. It is found on snowboard cross courses.

Big Air
A snowboarding event where the rider is judged on how high the board is off the ground, the difficulty of the move, and how well he or she lands.

Carving
A high-speed turn on the edge of a snowboard.

ESPN
A television channel that broadcasts entertainment and sports programming.

Hotdogs
A rider who performs wild tricks on a snowboard.

Rail
A metal sliding surface that a snowboarder jumps onto and travels down its length.

Rollers
Small hills on a snowboard cross track.

Shredder
A skilled snowboarder.

Slalom
A downhill race that sends the snowboarder between sets of poles called "gates." Giant slalom has more gates and the course is steeper than regular slalom. Parallel slalom is a head-to-head race between two snowboarders going down side-by-side courses marked with gates and flags.

Snowboard Cross
A head-to-head race between 4 to 6 snowboarders on a course that features many turns and jumps.

Snowboard Street
A competition where riders perform jumps and tricks across walls and down railings.

Superpipe
A large U-shaped snow structure with nearly vertical walls that are 22 feet (6.7 m) tall.

X Games
Extreme sporting events, such as snowboard competitions, that are broadcast each year in the summer and winter by the ESPN television network.

INDEX